MY FAVORITE CLOTHES

by Pearl Markovics

Consultant:
Beth Gambro
Reading Specialist
Yorkville, Illinois

Contents

My Favorite Clothes........2
Key Words 16
Index......................16
About the Author 16

New York, New York

My Favorite Clothes

What do you love?

I love clothes!

I love big hats.

What do you love?

What do you love?

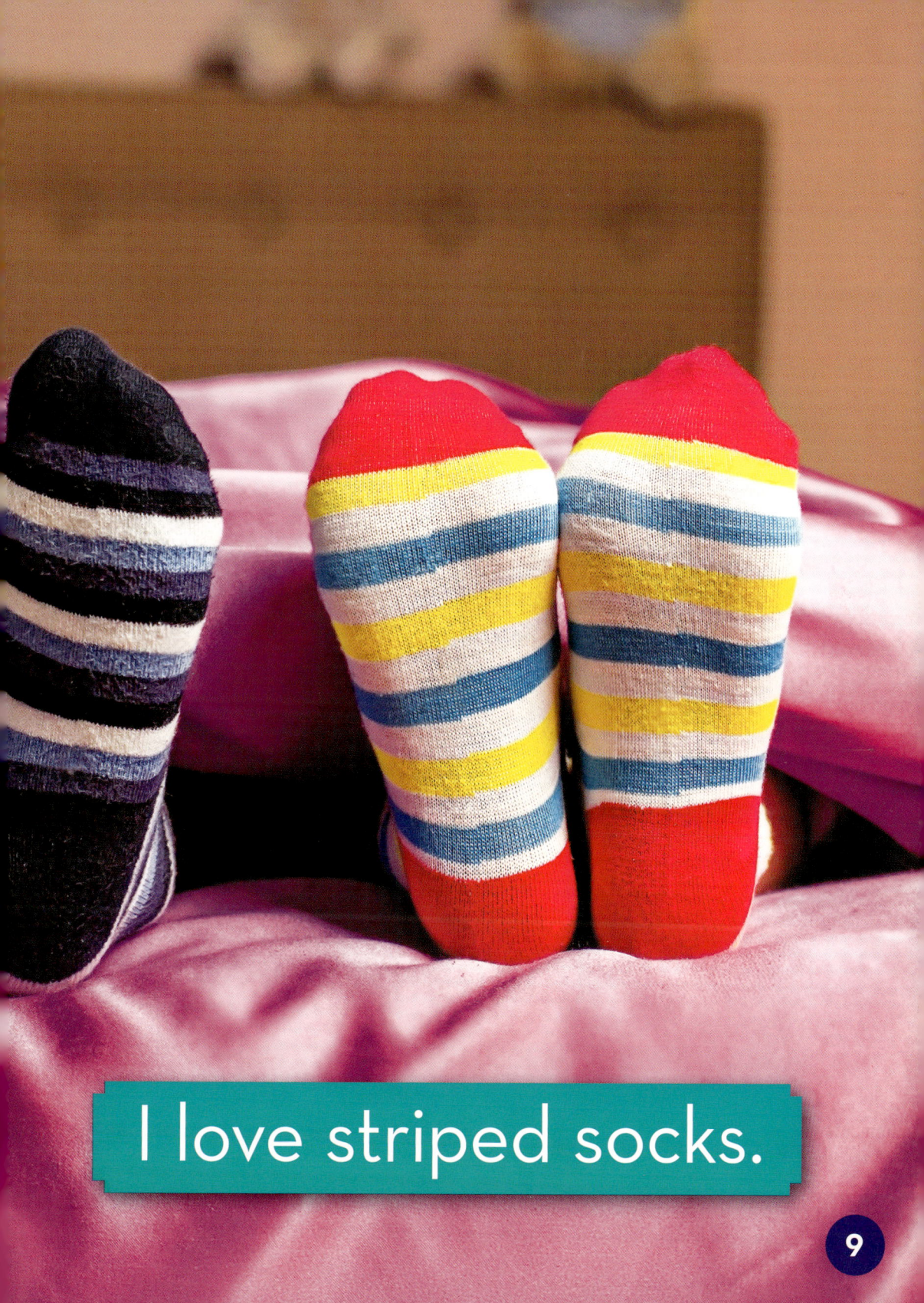

I love striped socks.

What do you love?

I love warm mittens.

What do you love?

I love spotted pajamas.

Pick your favorite!

Key Words

hats

mittens

pajamas

shirts

socks

Index

hats 4–5   pajamas 12–13   socks 8–9
mittens 10–11   shirts 6–7

About the Author

Pearl Markovics has many favorite things. The piece of clothing she loves most of all is a black T-shirt!